WOULD YOU RATHER...

BUNGEE JUMP HOLDING A PORCUPINE

~OR~

SKYDIVE HOLDING A SKUNK?

BE 9 MONTHS OLD

~OR~

1,080 MONTHS OLD?

WOULD YOU RATHER...

BEGIN EVERY SENTENCE WITH "ACCORDING TO MY KNOWLEDGE"

END EVERY SENTENCE WITH "JUST KIDDING"?

DRINK A BOTTLE OF SEA WATER

A CUP OF CLEAN TOILET WATER?

WOULD YOU RATHER....

BREAK THE MOST VALUABLE THING IN YOUR OWN HOUSE

THE MOST VALUABLE THING AT THE ANTIQUE STORE?

BE A PIRATE WITHOUT A SHIP

BE A NINJA WITH SQUEAKY SHOES?

WOULD YOU RATHER....

SIT IN THE AIRPLANE BETWEEN TWO ARGUING PASSENGERS

 ~OR~

NEXT TO A SCREAMING TODDLER?

HAVE A DOG THAT COULD HUM

 ~OR~

A CAT THAT COULD WHISTLE?

WOULD YOU RATHER...

EAT CHOCOLATE-FLAVORED POO

~OR~

POO-FLAVORED CHOCOLATE?

BE A SLOW TIGER

~OR~

A VERY FAST SLOTH?

WOULD YOU RATHER...

CRY RAINBOW-COLORED TEARS

FART RAINBOW-COLORED BUBBLES?

BE A GIRAFFE WITH NECK PAIN

A HIPPO WITH AN ALLERGY TO DIRT?

WOULD YOU RATHER...

SHOOT SPAGHETTI OUT OF YOUR INDEX FINGERS

~OR~

SNEEZE MEATBALLS?

ALWAYS TALK IN RHYMES

~OR~

SING INSTEAD OF SPEAK?

WOULD YOU RATHER...

GET ALL A'S IN SCHOOL WITHOUT TRYING BUT LEARN NOTHING

GET C'S WHILE TRYING HARD BUT LEARN A LOT?

BE ON AN EMPTY BEACH WHEN IT'S CLOUDY

ON A CROWDED BEACH WHEN IT'S SUNNY?

WOULD YOU RATHER...

CALL A RANDOM NUMBER AND INITIATE A CONVERSATION

SUDDENLY HUG A STRANGER ON THE STREET?

CUT GRASS WITH YOUR TEETH

WASH THE DISHES WITH YOUR TONGUE?

WOULD YOU RATHER....

LIVE IN A CARTOON WORLD WHERE YOU ARE THE ONLY REAL PERSON

LIVE IN A REAL WORLD WHERE YOU ARE A CARTOON?

FALL INTO A PUDDLE OF MUD

FALL INTO YELLOW SNOW?

WOULD YOU RATHER...

COUNT EVERY GRAIN OF SAND IN A SANDBOX

COUNT EVERY DROP OF WATER IN THE POOL?

EAT NO CANDY FOR HALLOWEEN

NO TURKEY FOR THANKSGIVING?

WOULD YOU RATHER...

HAVE A 5-INCH LONG BELLY BUTTON THAT SWAYED TO MUSIC

~OR~

HAVE ACCORDIONS FOR LEGS?

CLEAN THE FLOOR WITH THE TOOTHBRUSH

~OR~

MOW THE LAWN WITH THE PAIR OF SCISSORS?

WOULD YOU RATHER...

HAVE THOUGHT BUBBLES APPEAR ABOVE YOUR HEAD SO EVERYONE CAN READ YOUR THOUGHTS

~OR~

EVERYONE YOU KNOW HAS ACCESS TO YOUR BROWSING HISTORY?

HAVE THE ABILITY TO TELEPORT EVERY TIME YOU BURP

~OR~

HEAL ANY WOUND BY JUST SCREAMING AT IT?

WOULD YOU RATHER...

GET CAUGHT EATING A BOOGER

SCRATCHING YOUR PRIVATES?

HAVE TO SLEEP WEARING A MOTORCYCLE HELMET

WEARING SKATES?

WOULD YOU RATHER...

GET TICKLED FOR TEN MINUTES

HAVE TO HOLD A TARANTULA FOR ONE MINUTE?

LISTEN TO JUSTIN BIEBER FOR THE REST OF YOUR LIFE

ONLY WATCH THE GOLF CHANNEL FOR THE REST OF YOUR LIFE?

WOULD YOU RATHER....

DRINK A GLASS OF FAT

SNORT A TABLESPOON OF SALT?

BE ABLE TO SPEAK DOLPHIN

READ BABIES' MINDS?

WOULD YOU RATHER...

IMPRESS YOUR MOM BY HELPING HER WITH THE DISHES

 ~OR~

BY BUYING HER A PRESENT?

HAVE A JEDI LIGHTSABER

 ~OR~

CAPTAIN AMERICA'S SHIELD?

WOULD YOU RATHER...

HAVE DISAPPOINTING CHRISTMAS PRESENTS

NO PRESENTS AT ALL?

BE STUCK ON A BROKEN FERRIS WHEEL

IN A BROKEN ELEVATOR?

WOULD YOU RATHER...

NOT BE ABLE TO CLOSE ANY DOOR ONCE IT'S OPEN

~OR~

NOT BE ABLE TO OPEN ANY DOOR ONCE IT'S CLOSED?

BE THE BEST VIDEOGAME PLAYER IN THE WORLD

~OR~

THE WORST BASKETBALL PLAYER IN THE NBA?

WOULD YOU RATHER...

WEAR WINTER COAT IN SUMMER

SUMMER SHIRT IN WINTER?

ALWAYS BE BUSY

ALWAYS BE BORED?

WOULD YOU RATHER...

GET LOCKED INSIDE A MOVIE THEATER

~OR~

GET LOCKED INSIDE A SUPERMARKET?

SOUND LIKE SIRI

~OR~

JAR-JAR BINKS FOR THE REST OF YOUR LIFE?

WOULD YOU RATHER...

HAVE THE LIGHTS ON

~OR~

OFF IF YOU KNEW THE ROOM WAS FULL OF SCORPIONS?

EXPLODE IF YOU DON'T CHECK INTO YOUR HOUSE BY MIDNIGHT EVERY DAY

~OR~

HAVE TO SLEEP SOMEPLACE NEW EVERY NIGHT?

WOULD YOU RATHER...

GET FLOUR IN YOUR FACE

AN EGG SMASHED OVER YOUR HEAD?

LIVE IN NARNIA

STUDY AT HOGWARTS?

WOULD YOU RATHER...

HAVE A DRAGON

BE A DRAGON?

HAVE A STICKY CELL PHONE

ITCHY PANTS?

WOULD YOU RATHER...

GET $5 EVERY TIME YOU EAT A CARROT

 ~OR~

$50 EVERY TIME YOU EAT A BIG MAC?

BE THE WORLD CHAMPION OF BOWLING

 ~OR~

THE WORLD CHAMPION OF ARCHERY?

WOULD YOU RATHER....

BE KNOWN AS A ONE-HIT WONDER FOR A BOOK

 ~OR~

FOR A SONG?

ALWAYS FEEL LIKE YOU'RE ABOUT TO SNEEZE

 ~OR~

ALWAYS FEEL LIKE YOU'RE ABOUT TO FART?

WOULD YOU RATHER...

GIVE A SPEECH IN FRONT OF THE WHOLE SCHOOL INCLUDING TEACHERS FOR AN HOUR

WORK IN THE SCHOOL CAFETERIA FOR A SEMESTER?

FORGET YOUR FAVORITE BOOK SO YOU CAN READ IT AGAIN FOR THE FIRST TIME

FORGET YOUR FAVORITE MOVIE SO YOU CAN WATCH IT FOR THE FIRST TIME?

WOULD YOU RATHER....

BE TELEPORTED TO RANDOM PLACES ON EARTH
WITH JUST YOUR WALLET

 ~OR~

JUST YOUR CLOTHES?

FORGET ALL OF THE BAD THINGS YOU HAVE DONE

 ~OR~

BE FORGIVEN FOR THEM?

WOULD YOU RATHER...

NEVER PLAY

~OR~

PLAY BUT ALWAYS LOSE?

BE STUCK ON A DESERT ISLAND ALONE

~OR~

WITH SOMEONE WHO TALKS INCESSANTLY?

WOULD YOU RATHER...

HAVE TWO LAZY EYES

~OR~

ALWAYS GET NOSE BLEEDS AT CRUCIAL MOMENTS?

WITNESS AN EPIC MOMENT IN HISTORY

~OR~

WITNESS AN EVENT FROM THE FUTURE?

WOULD YOU RATHER...

HAVE NO FINGERNAILS

~OR~

NAILS TWICE THE SIZE OF YOUR FINGER?

WIN A TRIP TO HAWAII

~OR~

WIN A VIDEO GAME CONSOLE?

WOULD YOU RATHER....

BE ABLE TO CUT BUSHES INTO ANIMAL SHAPES

~OR~

CARVE ICE SCULPTURES?

BE 4 FEET TALL

~OR~

BE 8 FEET TALL?

WOULD YOU RATHER...

BE ABLE TO SEE 15 MINUTES INTO YOUR OWN FUTURE

15 MINUTES INTO SOMEBODY ELSE'S FUTURE?

JUMP INTO A POOL OF STRAWBERRY PUDDING

A POOL OF CHOCOLATE ICE CREAM?

WOULD YOU RATHER...

HAVE TO WEAR WET SOCKS FOR THE REST OF YOUR LIFE

~OR~

ONLY BE ALLOWED TO BRUSH YOUR TEETH ONCE A YEAR?

HAVE YOUR FUTURE DECIDED BY A GROUP OF RANDOM PEOPLE

~OR~

BY AN AUTOMATED MACHINE?

WOULD YOU RATHER...

EAT SPAGHETTI THROUGH A STRAW

EAT SPAGHETTI BLENDED INTO A SMOOTHIE?

TAKE A PUNCH TO THE FACE FROM MIKE TYSON

A KICK TO THE HEAD FROM CONOR MCGREGOR?

WOULD YOU RATHER...

SPEND THE HOLIDAYS WITH YOUR FAMILY

WITH TWO CELEBRITIES OF YOUR CHOOSING?

GET BRAIN FREEZE FROM SOMETHING COLD

BURN YOUR TONGUE WITH SOMETHING HOT?

WOULD YOU RATHER...

WIN AN ARGUMENT

WIN A GAME?

GET RID OF ALL COCKROACHES

ALL MOSQUITOES?

WOULD YOU RATHER...

BE A FAITHFUL DOG

~OR~

A WILD FREE MONGOOSE?

BE TRAPPED IN AN ELEVATOR WITH A FIGHTING COUPLE

~OR~

A SUSPICIOUS CLOWN?

WOULD YOU RATHER...

HAVE A GUY

A GIRL AS YOUR BEST FRIEND?

FINISH 5 JARS OF JAM IN ONE GO

MAKE A 50 EGG OMELET?

WOULD YOU RATHER...

HAVE ONE EYE TWICE AS BIG AS THE OTHER

~OR~

ONE EAR TWICE AS BIG AS THE OTHER?

HAVE ARMS AS LONG AS YOUR FINGERS

~OR~

HAVE FINGERS AS LONG AS YOUR ARMS?

WOULD YOU RATHER...

BLINK AT TWICE THE NORMAL RATE

YAWN EVERY MINUTE?

HAVE TO GROW YOUR OWN FOOD

EAT ONLY MCDONALD'S FOOD EVERY DAY?

WOULD YOU RATHER...

GET PAINFUL PIMPLES ON YOUR BUTT

ON YOUR NOSE?

HAVE A HIGHER IQ

A PHOTOGRAPHIC MEMORY?

WOULD YOU RATHER...

BE ABLE TO SPEAK WITH YOUR PET

SPEAK WITH ONE ANIMAL SPECIES OF YOUR CHOOSING?

HAVE PERMANENTLY POINTY TEETH

HAVE PERMANENTLY BLOODSHOT EYES?

WOULD YOU RATHER...

BE PLAYING VIDEO GAMES ONE DAY BEFORE THE EXAM

PREPARING A CHEAT SHEET FOR THE EXAM?

BE KNOWN FOR SOMETHING REALLY BAD

DO SOMETHING REALLY GOOD BUT NO ONE WOULD KNOW ABOUT YOU?

WOULD YOU RATHER...

HAVE A SUPERPOWER YOU CAN'T TELL ANYONE ABOUT

HAVE A SUPERPOWER BUT NOT KNOW WHAT IT IS?

LIVE IN ANTARCTICA

THE SAHARA DESERT?

WOULD YOU RATHER...

HAVE BATMAN'S MONEY, SKILLS, EQUIPMENT, AND LIFESTYLE

END CRIME AROUND THE WORLD FOR GOOD BUT BE POOR AND UNKNOWN?

SMELL LIKE FISH EVERY TIME YOU STEP OUT OF THE SHOWER

SMELL LIKE POOP EVERY TIME YOU STEP OUT THE RESTROOM?

WOULD YOU RATHER...

BE LOST IN THE JUNGLE

~OR~

TRAVEL TO A BLACK HOLE?

BECOME A SCARY WITCH

~OR~

A HORRIFYING MUMMY FOR HALLOWEEN?

WOULD YOU RATHER...

FLIP A COIN FOR A CHANCE TO WIN $40

~OR~

IMMEDIATELY WIN $20?

BE THE BEST AT MATH

~OR~

THE BEST AT LANGUAGES?

WOULD YOU RATHER...

BECOME SOMEBODY ELSE

~OR~

JUST BE YOURSELF?

GIVE SOME RANDOM PERSON ACCESS TO YOUR SOCIAL MEDIA ACCOUNTS

~OR~

LOSE ALL THE DATA ON THOSE ACCOUNTS?

WOULD YOU RATHER...

ALWAYS FALL ASLEEP AT NINE PM AND WAKE UP AT SIX AM

ALWAYS FALL ASLEEP AT ONE AM AND WAKE UP AT TEN AM?

HAVE TWO BELLY BUTTONS

NO BELLY BUTTON?

WOULD YOU RATHER...

LIVE WITHOUT THE INTERNET

LIVE WITHOUT AIR CONDITIONING AND HEATING?

BLINDLY TOUCH SOMETHING

BLINDLY TASTE SOMETHING?

WOULD YOU RATHER...

BE ABLE TO SEE WITH YOUR EYES CLOSED

BE ABLE TO HEAR WITH YOUR EARS COVERED?

FORGET HOW TO RIDE A BIKE

FORGET HOW TO SPELL WORDS?

WOULD YOU RATHER...

HAVE A GIANT HEAD

~OR~

A HIGH PITCHED BABY VOICE?

HAVE MORE FREE TIME

~OR~

MORE MONEY?

WOULD YOU RATHER...

TURN INTO AN EAGLE FOR ONE DAY

TURN INTO A SHARK FOR ONE DAY?

WATCH HORROR MOVIES

MUSICALS FOR THE REST OF YOUR LIFE?

WOULD YOU RATHER...

EAT A BUG

~OR~

GET STUNG BY A BEE?

BEAT UP AN 8-YEAR-OLD

~OR~

BEAT UP AN 80-YEAR-OLD?

WOULD YOU RATHER...

NEVER HAVE TO BREATHE BUT ALWAYS FELT LIKE YOU WERE SUFFOCATING

~OR~

NEVER HAVE TO EAT BUT ALWAYS FELT HUNGRY?

MAKE PEOPLE LAUGH

~OR~

CRY BY JUST TOUCHING THEM?

WOULD YOU RATHER...

BE A MILLIONAIRE

~OR~

LIVE IN THE HOGWARTS CASTLE?

HAVE TEN STITCHES TO FIX A BAD CUT

~OR~

HAVE ONE TOOTH REMOVED?

WOULD YOU RATHER....

HAVE TO SING EVERY SENTENCE YOU SAY

HAVE TO READ OUT LOUD EVERY BOOK YOU READ?

HAVE A WITCH'S NOSE

VAMPIRE FANGS?

WOULD YOU RATHER...

HAVE A REMOTE CONTROL THAT MADE YOUR MOM STOP TALKING

~OR~

REMOTE CONTROL THAT MADE YOUR DAD STOP TALKING?

BE ABLE TO SING LIKE AN OPERA SINGER

~OR~

BE ABLE TO PLAY THE GUITAR LIKE A ROCK STAR?

WOULD YOU RATHER...

HAVE TO EAT A BOWL FULL OF ANTS

 ~OR~

A BOWL FULL OF WORMS?

WEAR EARPLUGS TO CLASS FOR A MONTH

 ~OR~

WEAR SUNGLASSES TO CLASS FOR A WHOLE SEMESTER?

WOULD YOU RATHER...

FALL OUT WITH YOUR FRIENDS

EVERYONE ELSE BUT THEM?

LOOK STRONG AND BE WEAK

LOOK WEAK AND BE STRONG?

WOULD YOU RATHER...

BE SURPRISED BY A GIFT

BE ABLE TO PICK WHAT YOU GET?

GIVE UP FACEBOOK

YOUTUBE?

WOULD YOU RATHER...

DRINK A GLASS OF BOILING WATER

TEACH 500 GRANDMAS HOW TO USE FACEBOOK?

HAVE THE POWER TO PUT OTHERS IN
EMBARRASSING SITUATIONS

HAVE THE POWER TO REMOVE YOURSELF FROM
EMBARRASSING SITUATIONS?

WOULD YOU RATHER...

SING A SONG IN FRONT OF STRANGERS

~OR~

IN FRONT OF YOUR CLOSEST FRIENDS?

BE ABLE TO TALK TO YOUR CAT(DOG)

~OR~

TO PEOPLE WHO ARE DEAD VIA TEXT MESSENGER?

WOULD YOU RATHER...

EAT AN ENTIRE BAG OF HOT DOGS

AN ENTIRE BAG OF HOT DOG BUNS?

HAVE FEET THAT KEPT GROWING AS YOU GOT OLDER

HANDS THAT KEPT GETTING SMALLER AS YOU GOT OLDER?

WOULD YOU RATHER...

TALK LIKE MASTER YODA

~OR~

BREATHE LIKE DARTH VADER?

BRUSH YOUR TEETH WITH WASABI

~OR~

WITH RANCH DRESSING?

WOULD YOU RATHER...

REVEAL YOUR BEST FRIENDS SECRET

JUMP INTO ICE-COLD WATER FOR A DARE?

HAVE THREE WISHES IN THREE YEARS

ONE WISH RIGHT NOW?

WOULD YOU RATHER...

BE ABLE TO CONTROL YOUR DREAMS

 ~OR~

BE ABLE TO RECORD YOUR DREAMS?

HAVE A MISSING FINGER

 ~OR~

THREE EXTRA FINGERS?

WOULD YOU RATHER...

RECEIVE 5 ANONYMOUS VALENTINE'S DAY CARDS

RECEIVE ONE VALENTINE'S DAY CARD BUT YOU KNOW WHO SENT IT?

STUDY ONLY ON HOLIDAYS

ONLY GET HOLIDAYS OFF SCHOOL?

WOULD YOU RATHER....

BE INVISIBLE AT A PARTY

~OR~

BE OBLIGATED TO ENTERTAIN EVERYONE AT A PARTY?

BE COMPLETELY INSANE AND KNOW THAT YOU ARE INSANE

~OR~

BE COMPLETELY INSANE AND BELIEVE YOU ARE SANE?

WOULD YOU RATHER....

HAVE TO WEAR ONLY UNCOMFORTABLE CLOTHES

~OR~

ONLY BE ABLE TO USE SCRATCHY THIN TOILET PAPER
FOR THE REST OF YOUR LIFE?

EAT ONLY JUNK FOOD

~OR~

ONLY FRUITS AND VEGETABLES FOR A MONTH?

WOULD YOU RATHER...

KISS YOUR BEST FRIEND'S ARMPIT

LET A RANDOM PERSON LICK YOU?

ALWAYS BE HUNGRY

ALWAYS BE TIRED?

WOULD YOU RATHER...

ALWAYS WAKE UP IN THE MIDDLE OF A NICE DREAM AND NOT BE ABLE TO FALL BACK TO SLEEP

 ~OR~

NEVER BE ABLE TO WAKE UP FROM A NIGHTMARE?

BE THE GUY WHO PUTS HIS HEAD IN THE LION'S MOUTH IN THE CIRCUS

 ~OR~

THE CLOWN WHO IS SHOT OUT OF A CANNON?

WOULD YOU RATHER...

PLANTS COULD TALK

ANIMALS COULD TALK?

BE A VOLCANO

A SPACESHIP?

WOULD YOU RATHER...

GROW A PERMANENT SANTA BEARD

~OR~

GROW PERMANENT REINDEER ANTLERS?

KEEP EASTER GET RID OF CHIRSTMAS

~OR~

KEEP CHIRSTMAS GET RID OF EASTER?

WOULD YOU RATHER....

MEET THE PRESIDENT OF THE USA

 ~OR~

YOUR FAVORITE ACTOR?

BE ABLE TO DISAPPEAR

 ~OR~

BE ABLE TO ERASE SOMEONE'S MEMORY?

WOULD YOU RATHER...

HAVE A BATH OF SLUGS

 ~OR~

A SHOWER OF SPIDERS?

BE FAMOUS

 ~OR~

BE THE BEST FRIEND OF SOMEONE FAMOUS?

WOULD YOU RATHER...

TURN INTO AN EAGLE FOR ONE DAY

~OR~

TURN INTO A SHARK FOR ONE DAY?

HAVE TO WEAR A GIANT BUNNY COSTUME

~OR~

A GIANT EASTER EGG COSTUME?

YOUR REVIEW

I HOPE YOU'VE ENJOYED READING THIS LITTLE BOOK. AND IT WOULD BE GREAT IF YOU COULD TAKE A MOMENT OF YOUR TIME TO WRITE DOWN A SHORT REVIEW ON THE BOOK'S AMAZON PAGE. YOUR FEEDBACK IS VERY IMPORTANT TO ME. IT WILL ALSO HELP OTHERS TO MAKE AN INFORMED DECISION BEFORE PURCHASING THIS BOOK. THANK YOU IN ADVANCE,

- DAN GILDEN

Made in the USA
Monee, IL
06 April 2020